Total Zone Play

Concepts

Space
Time
Shifting
Transition

7 : ∞

3 : ∞

First Edition

ISBN: 978-1-304-40012-3

Table of Contents

Introduction

This book is a conceptual approach to the zone play. In this book, the fundamental concepts of the zone are analyzed that, in my opinion, are the basis of this type of play. In other specialized resources published on this subject, the authors present this topic with particular attention paid to the non-possession phase of play – namely, zone defence as opposed to man-to-man or mixed defensive versions.

Andre Villas-Boas, in an interview for UEFA's magazine, *The Technician*, was asked what the most important trends in top football were today. He answered,

> No doubt the game speed, speed decision making and speed of the counterattacks. But, the exception to the rule is FC Barcelona. Barcelona's players can play at full speed as the other teams' players but they have something special: they have a talent for space and time. They have redefined how to play football creating more time for possession and taking players' decision making to another level. What Guardiola did at Barcelona was to redefine the notions of space and time keeping circulation of the ball and the rest of the game fast.

Arrigo Sacchi once said in an interview, "I have seen three great teams in my lifetime: the Ajax and Holland side of the 1970s; my Milan at the end of the 1980s; and today Barcelona with Pep Guardiola at the helm."

"Total football", as Rinus Michels' system came to be known, made an enemy of rigidity. Until his sides showed the world another way, football teams had largely relied on strict formations with lines of players strung across the field like the wooden figures in a bar-football game. Michels' players were given freedom to swap positions at will, with defenders allowed and encouraged to join the attack. Every player was expected to be supremely comfortable in possession of the football and to be able to adapt to any role.

Again in an interview, Arrigo Sacchi said, "There has been only one real tactical revolution, and it happened when football shifted from an individual to a collective game. It happened with Ajax first and then the Holland national team at the beginning of the 1970s. For Johan Cruyff and the rest of the Dutch players, the field suddenly became small; for the other teams, the field remained enormously big." After that, coaches started looking for ways to improve and develop their tactics. Playing man-to-man was gradually replaced by zone play or mixed zone play. Polyvalent profile players who had the ability to play in different areas became preferred over those players who only played one position. The vast majority of systems at that time were derived from the new type of organization: the zone. These principles and concepts were quickly assimilated and adapted to the national characteristics and philosophies of each football club. Emergent game rules – such as pass back to the goalkeeper, red card for the last defender, and three points for a win – changed technical and tactical principles and therefore the methods of training.

By analyzing the evolution of the football game in recent years and taking as a reference the playing style of FC Barcelona in particular, one could say that the coaches' vision has been hugely important in terms of game development, and there is still much of their vision that remains unexplored. My desire to find answers to questions regarding game development stems from my personal experience with Manchester United and Ajax Amsterdam, and it was fuelled by what I learned while taking part in various courses at FA and while watching UAE coaches with extensive football experience. I found that the zone play offers unlimited possibilities for game development.

Purpose

The knowledge gained during my work as a coach, my time conducting match analysis from different perspectives, and my enrolment in specialized football courses led me to hone in on three game-oriented matters I want to address. I will be

a) detailing the four fundamental concepts of zone play;

b) designing training methods and drills to coach the zone play while in possession of the ball; and

c) arguing why we should introduce zone play concepts to children and juniors in their daily training.

Hypotheses

If the principles and concepts of zone play are introduced and adapted as early as possible in children's and juniors' training, then the players will gain a better understanding of playing in the zone.

Zone Play

What does zone play mean? In the zone play, the players are moving according to the ball position both defensively and, in my opinion, offensively. Depending on the position of the ball, players are primarily responsible for a certain area of the field, and they are also responsible for opposing players entering that area. The players share their tasks in their tactical area when they have to cover a common area but without crossing their movements.

Horizontal and vertical shifting can decrease or increase the distance between the lines and compartments. During the shift, in the phase of non-possession, players have to maintain their positions in the defensive line and move with the entire defensive module into another area of the field, depending on the ball position. Herman Vermeulen, in his book *Zone Soccer*, states, "Zone football is not an exact science but rather a philosophy of play. The zone is the game based on the ball position."

When did people speak for the first time about zone play? The zone play is a philosophy developed by coaches thinking tactically during the era of man-to-man playing. Coaches and especially players were confronted with a number of tactical situations, and effective solutions had to be found for the teams to win.

Examples:

The line of four defenders was organized to play with a marking player and a sweeper, which often led to situations of inconsistency between the tasks of the two players. Midfielders were mainly concerned about their direct opponents and then about the ball. Strikers had reduced tasks during the phase of defending. The speed of play, the presence of very good opponents in one-on-one duels, and continuous movement of the players created tactical problems to those teams that relied on man-to-man play. A first step towards adopting the zone organization was to develop an intermediate form of organization – namely man-to-man play in the zone, which can especially apply to set pieces. Of course, the game has evolved tactically, and some coaches have chosen a pure zone play organization in which man-to-man marking becomes almost nonexistent.

Zone play does not exclude marking, double marking, or any other tactical action present in the man-to-man type of organization, but they are used under other conditions specific to zone play. Each form of organization has advantages and disadvantages. Often coaches reasoned that they could not switch to zone play because their players were not suited to the technical and tactical requirements of zone play; the most difficult change was the reorganization of the defensive line.

The transition from one marking player and a sweeper to four players in line, or from five players (two marking players and a sweeper) to four players, created many debates, and coaches had to come up with new methods of training and thinking.

Main Differences between Zone Play and Man-to-Man:

In zone play, the focus is mainly on the ball position and the tactical area in which the actions take place, and then secondarily on the opposing players entering into that tactical space. The zone is a complex ensemble whose participants can develop many tactical ideas – unlike man-to-man, which limits individual ideas in terms of tactics. Differences exist during the ball possession phase as well, namely vertical and horizontal shifting of the players depending on the position and movement of the ball.

Background Study

Data collected during my time at FC Otelul Galati Football Academy (1995–2002), Manchester United Soccer School in Dubai (2007–2009), and Ajax Amsterdam Academy in Dubai (2010–2011) had an important role in the inception of this book. At Manchester United Academy I had the freedom to include in the U12 training plan my own drills and methods based on the concepts of zone play. In each practice I included at least one exercise that was based on one of these four zone play concepts. For example, an exercise of possession of the ball could be organized in various ways: possession in transition situations, possession conditioned by space and time, or possession with shifting objectives included.

The methods and exercises presented in this study are based on the feedback obtained during practice. Some drills have been modified from the organization and content point of view, to be tailored to the characteristics of the players.

In terms of my experience gained with Ajax Amsterdam, I can say that I was impressed by the attention that coaches gave to positional play and how this developed from the U9 to the first team.

Zone Play Concepts

The first contact children have with organized football usually occurs at the age of nine or ten, and sometimes even younger. At this age children learn the basic techniques and tactics of football. Indirectly, they are exposed to situations where a phase of the game is solved out through a good understanding and the application of zone play concepts: space, time, transition, and shifting.

Pep Guardiola said, "The best technique is when you have time and space to apply it." Including specific zone play concepts in the juniors' training is the challenge for the next generation of coaches. As the football game evolves, top teams will gain worldwide fame, and their styles and philosophies of play will inspire future generations of young footballers who are part of that club's academy. If you want to train young players to play the way the senior team plays, you must prepare them for this purpose at an early stage. The training philosophy of the club should be visible in all directions, from seniors to children and from children to seniors. For example, Ajax Amsterdam was the first team whose style of play clearly influenced the development of the young academy players.

What is the best age to introduce specific zone play concepts in the juniors training? How do these young players make the transition to the first team if, in their previous experience, they were not trained on the principles of zone play? Could training be tailored to youth characteristics so that they gain an understanding of the zone play at the very beginning of their football experiences?

Below are some of the questions that I am going to answer in the following chapters.

Zone Play Concepts – Training Methods and Exercises

- What is the meaning of these concepts during everyday practice?
- How do we transfer these concepts from practice to game and from game to practice?
- Do we design training methods for each separate concept, or do we adapt existing resources to the demands of zone play?
- How can we facilitate the introduction and adaptation of these concepts according to the age and development characteristics of juniors?

The methods of training must meet certain general requirements to be effective (Michels, Rinus 2001, 221).

- To be a real tactical problem based on an official match analysis
- To have clear objectives to be understood by the players
- To be organized from the beginning to the end without losing time that will influence players' motivation
- To be challenging and to give coherence and meaning to exercise
- To be presented visually before being applied in practice
- To simulate real-game situations so as to be easily recognized by players

The Concept of Space in the Game of Football

Space and time are two basic concepts of the zone play. At the ages of six to nine years old, children do not understand space and time in the sense that experienced players understand it. Basics such as field orientation and the perception of distances between players, between players and ball, and between players and the goal, can be introduced at an early stage. Children gradually begin to perceive the spatial aspects of length, width, backwards, forwards, or sideways. As a result of the ball's and players' movements, this space changes continuously in shape and size.

In fact, at this age children perceive the space, but they can't see the change of these spatial cues, which are fast moving in a football match. They often remain in the space of a previous phase over a long period of time, until they notify the changes in space.

In the football game the meaning of space is:

A) The distance between one player and his opponents

B) The distance between one player and his teammates

C) The distance between one player and the ball

D) The distance between one player and the sidelines

E) The distance between one player and the goal (own or opposition's)

Continuous movements of the ball and players create this free space for shorter or longer periods of time in certain areas of the field. Giovanni Trapattoni said, "The main problem that we had to solve when our team had possession of the ball was to create space, to seek and to position themselves in different areas of the field, using that free area for the team's advantage."

Barry Hulshoff, a former Ajax teammate of Cruyff, said,

> We discussed space all the time. Cruyff always talked about where people should run, where they should stand, where they should not be moving. It was all about making space and coming into space. It is a kind of architecture on the field. It is about movement, but still it is about space, about organizing space. You have to know why building up from the right side or from the left side is different movement from when you build up from the centre. We always talked about speed of ball, space and time. Where is the most space? Where is the player who has the most time? That is where we have to play the ball. Every player had to understand the whole geometry of the whole pitch and the system as a whole.

FC Barcelona midfielder Xavi Hernandez said, "Think quickly, look for spaces. That's what I do: look for spaces. All day. I'm always looking. All day, all day. [Xavi starts gesturing as if he is looking around, swinging his head.] Here? No. There? No. People who haven't played don't always realize how hard that is. Space, space, space. It's like being on the PlayStation."

Match analysis of those teams playing zone show that a great positional distribution on the field, developed in relation to the position of the ball, happens when the players receive the ball in space. The distance between the attacker who receives the ball and his direct defender is in most of the cases five metres or more. This receiving distance enables the attacker to avoid contact with the opponent and thus provides a prolonged period of time for analysis and decision making. A continuous positioning of the players in the receiving space is an action prepared in advance, anticipating the possibility of developing the game in that particular area. The first spatial reference point taken into consideration by the players, when they are positioning in the receiving area, is the distance to the nearest defender or defenders. This receiving distance changes during the game, especially in the active area around the ball, and therefore permanent adjustment of this distance is a prerequisite for maintaining the space.

Guardiola "distinguishes two types of demarcation: the demarcation to maintain possession of the ball and demarcation to attack opposing space".

Mourinho about space: "logic geometrical layout that allows the development of the game".

Game analysis of FC Barcelona with regards to positional play, namely receiving distance:

For instance, take a look at FC Barcelona–Athletic Bilbao, in the first half.

First half	Nr. of passes	0-1m	1-2m	2-3m	3-4m	4-5m	5m+
1-15'	80	3	10	14	10	9	32
15-30'	58	5	7	9	7	4	25
30-45'	92	3	12	11	9	5	52
Total	230	11	29	34	26	18	109

It is clearly seen that the players most often receive the ball when they have a distance of at least five metres to the nearest opponent. The placement of the players in a non-contact space inside the opponent's system is an indicator of the high training level of the positional game. Pep Guardiola said,

> The Italians told me it was hard to play football in Italy as the space was so limited in Italy ... I never understood this. How is there less space? In Italy, the fields are as big as in Spain or Holland. I found that the reason the game was lacking space, was

because the players moved wrong in relation to others. The reason space was limited was the lack of tactical ability of coaches and players.

Training Methods and Exercises for the Concept of Space

Starting at young ages, the players can develop their spatial orientation and correct perception of the distance between themselves and other conditioning factors of the game: ball, teammates, opponents, own goal, opposition goal, and sidelines. The space is also a conditioning factor when learning basic football techniques and tactics.

Exercise 1:

- Game is five versus five; pitch is divided into two equal sides.
- In own half, play with two touches; in the opposition's half, use free play.
- Players should always know where they are positioned on the field, and they should restrict their number of touches according to their position.

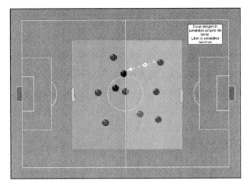

Exercise 2:

- Game is five versus five; field is divided into three vertical zones (right, left, centre).
- Free play touches on the sides and two touches in the central area.
- This game gives players the opportunity to improve their depth field orientation and to choose the right technique depending on the area of the field they are in at that moment.

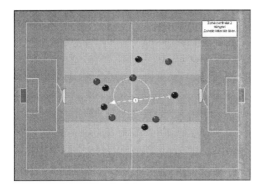

Exercise 3:

- Play five versus five; the field is divided into two vertical zones (left, right).
- No restrictions on the number of touches, but to score a goal, the players have to change the direction of play twice. The ball must go over the vertical line from the left to the right at least twice.

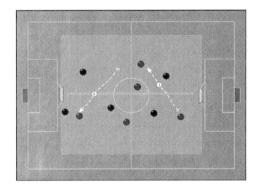

- The players have to change the direction of play, from one area to another, through combinations involving proper choice of technique depending on the area of the field, and they must find the right time to do it in relation to the game situation.

Exercise 4:

- Play a five versus five game; the playing field is divided into three horizontal zones.
- After each pass, the player must advance into the next horizontal zone, corresponding to the direction of attack; this exercise develops vertical space orientation and creates deep space towards the opposing goal.

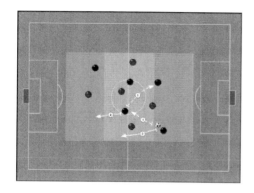

Exercise 5:

- Play five versus five, 40/30 metres, tag football.
- In this game there is no tackling. The defenders can win the ball if they tag the player who has possession. This exercise develops field orientation, having as point of reference the direct opponent or any other defenders in that area.
- The focus is on receiving the ball in space at a distance of at least four to five metres from the nearest opponent.

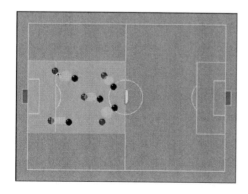

Exercise 6:

- Play five versus five, 40/30 metres, two areas of field, zonal progressive possession.

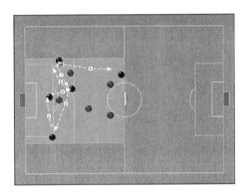

If the ball is recovered in their own half of the court, the team must maintain possession of the ball in this area and make at least five passes, in order to advance in the opponent's court. There is conditioning zonal progression by the number of passes the players have to accomplish in relation to the area of the field where the interception took place. If the ball is recovered in the opposing half of the field, continue to play unconditionally.

Shourin Roy wrote on his blog about "The man behind Louis Van Gaal".

> The hierarchical sense of football was turned on its head. In its place was what they would call in cybernetic parlance, a parallel distributed process. It allowed for speedier responses to changes in spatial demands, i.e., the expansion and collapse of space. The continuum of the game was dictated by which player would have the best access to that space,

either by a pass, or an intercept. It made no difference in the division of labour whether he was a striker, a full back, or a midfielder. There was a constant switching of positions.

The Concept of Time in the Game of Football

Time is a dimension of the game that does not seem to be visible in the early stages of development of children. A number of questions are raised about this concept. How do players perceive the time in different game situations? Can this component be coached in training? What are the moments of the game for which the time factor is decisive? What are the actions conditioned by time in the game of football? What is the best time, tactically speaking, for an action? A smooth succession of phases of play is also regarded as an excellent synchronization in time.

Johan Cruyff said, "Football is simple. You are in time or too late. When you are too late, you should start sooner. In small space, a player has to be capable of acting quickly. A good player who needs too much time can suddenly become a poor player."

"More and more teams are using at international level the principles of zone play. Football in the zone is an efficient use of time and space" (Vermeulen 2003, cover).

Time in the game of football can be expressed by:

1. Time of possession

2. Time the player has possession until tackled by an opponent

3. Time to react to different game situations

4. Time the ball moves from one player to another

5. Transition time (4 sec)

6. Time to recover the ball (6 sec)

7. Tempo and rhythm of the game

Time in the game of football is generally perceived by the score on the field at that time. A negative score gives players the feeling of running out of time, especially when the game is close to the end. This perception of time depending on the result makes the players actions become inappropriate and ineffective, and lacking in clarity.

Another time perception may be related to the duration of possession of the ball. A prolonged possession of the ball is a form of domination of the game, where the time is in favour of that team. The players use this strategy when their team is in advantage and want to keep the result during the remaining time of the game.

Also, the concept of time could be analyzed in terms of timing of the attacking actions (temporization) or the anticipation of the development of the game (typical situations). When a typical game phase is followed by another typical phase, between these two moments of the game there is a neutral time, called transition time, which connects these two game situations. This time of transition is a critical factor in solving tactical situations, knowing that the vast majority of goal opportunities are created as a result of this time discordance during two successive phases.

Time cannot be compressed or expanded, but its perception can be trained and directed depending on the tactical purpose of the game. Training resources can be adapted to train perception of time, both in terms of time compression and extension. The current trend is that players make decisions quickly so as to destabilize the organization of the defensive system and take advantage of the slow reactions of the opposing team. However, other teams, such as FC Barcelona, show that prolonged possession gives players the opportunity to wait for the right time for a deep pass and a vertical attack of the free space behind the defensive line – a decision that is made after a collective delay through keeping possession of the ball. Guardiola states, "We do not pass the ball for the sake of passing, but the purpose of long possession is to create free man and spaces in opposing defences. If space is not created then we pass it and pass it again."

FC. Barcelona – FC. Sevilla	Total number of passes	Passes forward	Passes backwards	Conclusions
45 min (first half)	300	180	120	40% of passes are against the direction of attack.

Training Methods and Exercises for the Concept of Time

Exercise 1:

- Play a five versus five. Players are conditioned by the contact time they can have with ball at their feet (no more than five seconds). Usually, players are conditioned during training by the number of touches of the ball (e.g., two-touch play), which sometimes limits the creativity of the players.
- By limiting the contact time with the ball, the players have the freedom to use as many touches as they want, but it must be done within that time limit.

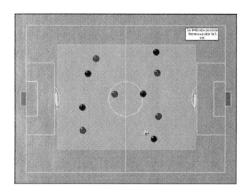

Exercise 2:

- Play a five versus five game. If a goal has been scored, the team that scored must maintain

28

possession of the ball for a certain period of time (e.g., one minute), after which they can finalize again.

- This training drill quantifies possession of the ball as duration in time and not as number of touches or passes. Usually during practice the players have a certain number of consecutive passes to accomplish, and this is an indication of a prolonged possession. If players are required to maintain possession of the ball for three minutes and not for ten consecutive passes, than the reaction to such a game conditioning will be quite different.
- Attention will be focused more on maintaining possession itself and less on the number of passes or touches they need to work on.

Exercise 3:

- Play a seven versus seven, with collective recovery of the ball in four seconds.
- This type of conditioning will lead to a rapid response from the players when they lose possession of the ball; this is a common goal achieved by all players. It is a training tool that prompts players to take part in overcoming their effort and psychological barriers specific to this type of high-intensity exercise.

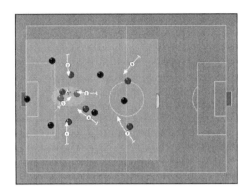

Exercise 4:

- Play a five versus five game.
- Create in practice a realistic scenario that improves players' responses to results pressure when running out of time. One team will be given five minutes, during which they must score three goals. Players must respond effectively to such a common situation when the result and the time left of the game create a huge pressure on the players. This perception of shortage of time in the game has to be managed by all the players for their own benefit, the most significant example being the end of the game in basketball where the last seconds can be decisive.
- When players are under pressure of a negative score, the tendency is that, in the last five minutes, they choose the simplest solutions with long balls thrown in the box, the goalkeeper coming in the box for set pieces, or a lack of calm in simple scoring opportunities.
- All these inefficient solutions taken under pressure may be changed by introducing practice drills with

limited playing time in which players must complete a game task.

The Concept of Shifting in the Game of Football

What is the ratio between horizontal shifting and vertical shifting in an official football game? Is shifting vertically a decisive factor in the game economy that needs attention?

Massimo Lucchesi, in his book *Pressing,* defines shifting as "a movement made by one or more players involved in the defence phase, who, following the team's strategies, its individual or collective tactical principles, move away from the original position on the playing field and go to take up another that is more useful from a tactical point of view" (Lucchesi 2003, 8). In playing zone, the players move according to the position of the ball. For each movement of the ball, there is a corresponding movement of the players called shifting. This concept is applicable both in the defence and in attack phases. Moving the ball on the ground's horizontal line requires in-zone play, a horizontal movement of the players. Moving the ball on the ground's vertical axis requires a vertical movement of the players in correspondence with the movement of the ball.

In correspondence with the movement of the ball on the ground's horizontal or vertical lines, the players are required to shift their positions accordingly. Paolo Maldini remarks, "Before Sacchi came to Milan, the clash between two opposing players was always the key, but with him it was all about movement off the ball, and that's where we won our matches."

Phase of Non-possession (Defence)

A game situation when the players are in their own half of the field, organized in defence against a positional attack, best reflects the horizontal shifting of a team depending on the ball position. Keeping lines compact during shifting on a lateral ball results in the release of an area of the field on the opposite side of the ball's position. When the ball is in the centre of the field, the teams use a pyramidal arrangement, thereby releasing the sides of the field.

Vertical shifting of a team during non-possession phase is best evidenced in situations where the defensive line clears an opposition's attack from the defending third. At this point, the defensive block moves out at twenty-five metres from its own goal in order to minimize the distances between lines, thus creating density in the area where the ball was cleared. A mobile team will create territory and numerical superiority, which will lead to superior self-confidence, allowing players to take initiative and express themselves on the pitch.

Training the non-possession phase begins with teaching the defensive line's shift, and then the midfielders and forwards will be added. Finally, we obtain a functional and compact team that is mobile and reactive to game situations.

Arrigo Sacchi said, "It is not a question of 4-4-2 or 4-2-1-3, it is a question of having a team which is ordered, in which the players are connected to one another, which moves together, as if it was a single player. Today few teams know how to do this. Few teams work as a unit – few, really few teams. They are all made up of little groups. There is no great connection, nor a good distribution of players around the pitch."

Phase of Possession (Attack)

If we analyze the methods and drills of training shifting during non-possession phase, I would say that there are no similar training methods that coaches can use to train shifting during possession phase. Besides tactical schemes in attack, with or without opponents, and attacking combinations drills with reduced number of players (one on one, three on three), the majority of the teams does not have a realistic possession and attack training method, according to the principles of the zone play.

In these training sessions, players must fully exploit the space they have when they enter the horizontal and vertical shifting depending on the ball position. Maintaining possession of the ball is not possible without adequate support from players of adjacent lines. When playing zone, continuous positioning of the players is required to keep possession of the ball, and this positioning is determined by the movement of the ball and opponents.

Typical situations are those game patterns that will be met in every match, and they are repeated unconditionally. During a game, we can differentiate about 100–150 typical game situations; each team organizes and trains these typical situations differently. All these tactical responses to typical situations will ultimately create the team's style and philosophy of playing.

The teams with good control of the game will create and train these typical situations and lead the game in a certain direction in their own tactical advantage.

Training Methods and Exercises for the Concept of Shifting

In the zone play, the movement of the players is depending on the position of the ball in both, attack and defence phase. For every move of the ball there is a corresponding movement of the players called shifting.

Phase of Possession (Attack)

During the building-up stage from the back and positional attack in the opposition's half, the team supports the player with the ball by horizontal or vertical shifting of the entire functional settlement. Here are some examples of horizontal shifting during phase of possession.

Typical situations:

A) The ball is at the goalkeeper

B) The ball is at the defenders' line

C) The ball is at the midfielders' line

D) The ball is at the strikers' line

Here are examples of vertical shifting during phase of possession.

Typical situation:

A) Ball movement on the right flank forwards/backwards

B) Ball movement on the left flank forwards/backwards

C) Ball movement on the centre forwards/backwards

D) Ball movement diagonally in depth forward/backwards

Horizontal Sifting

A) When the Goalkeeper Has the Ball

What are the players doing when the goalkeeper receives the ball and starts building up the game from the back? How does the whole functional system react?

Training Methods

Exercise 1:

- Horizontal shifting during phase of possession when the ball is at the goalkeeper (11 versus 11).
- Team is deployed in positional attack in the middle third.
- Opposing team's pressing forces a pass back to the goalkeeper.
- Horizontal shifting in front of their own penalty box, creating opportunities to receive the ball from the goalkeeper.

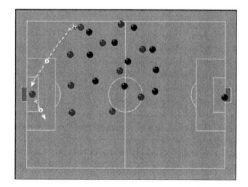

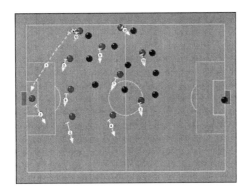

Exercise 2:

- Horizontal shifting, playing from the keeper.
- Play five versus two, with two small goals at the halfway line (or one target player)
- Four defenders and one midfielder against two attackers, positioned around the centre line; the ball is sent to the goalkeeper.
- Horizontal shifting to provide options for playing from the goalie.
- The midfielder drops back in the central area and participates in the horizontal shifting movement in relation to the ball, providing necessary support to the goalkeeper.

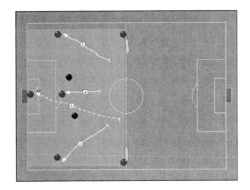

B) When the Ball Is in the Line with the Defenders

How does the team play when the ball is at one of the four defenders? What is the reaction of the goalkeeper? How do the other defenders support the game? What are the midfielders and strikers, who are positioned in front of the ball, doing?

When the ball is at one of the four defenders (back four), in the middle third of the field, it is possible to pass back to the goalkeeper, who supports the game by moving left or right and then he switches play to the other side. Defenders may offer through their positioning, with advanced full backs and withdrawn central defenders, an option to pass the ball along the defenders' line. This requires a good movement coordination of each of the four defenders.

During horizontal shifting the midfielders, depending on the position of the ball, are looking for space offered by the opposing team.

Strikers in horizontal shifting always seek the necessary space to receive the ball either in front of the opponents or behind them. A good positioning play offers the defenders

39

the possibility to pass the ball directly to the attackers through the midfielders' line.

Training Methods

Exercise 1:

- Phase of possession.
- Middle third of the field.
- The ball is passed from player to player along by the back four line.
- There is a neutral area for the defenders where they can be closed down but cannot be tackled.

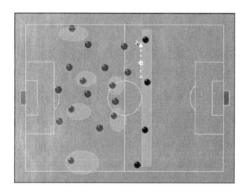

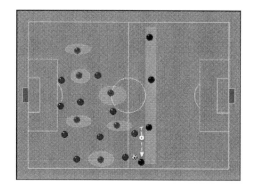

- Defenders: positioning, movement depending on the ball position and opposing players.
- Midfielders and forwards: positioning and movement in relation to the ball's position.
- Midfielders and strikers: positioned most of the time with their backs to the opposing goal.

Exercise 2:

- Isolated, no opposition except the mannequins.
- Ten mannequins positioned in a 4-3-3 system.

41

- Ball is in lateral movement between defensive line players (back four); midfielders and strikers move horizontally, depending on the position and movement of the ball, creating space in front of the ball.
- *For each movement of the ball, there is a corresponding movement of the players.*

Exercise 3:

- Phase of play, semi-active opponents (eleven versus eleven).
- Ball in lateral movement between the defensive line players.
- Opposing team is positioned in different organizational forms (e.g., 4-4-2).
- When the opposing team is positioned on the field in relation to the ball position, stop the game and ask the four midfielders and two strikers to position themselves in the space provided by the opposing team placement, at a distance of three to five metres from each opponent.

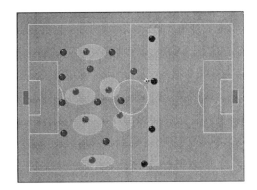

Exercise 4:

- Ball movement between the back four defenders for five seconds.
- Players of advanced lines enter the horizontal shifting, maintaining the distance between them and opposing players (three to five metres minimum distance that gives freedom of play).
- Stop and reassess the distances they had in initial positions.

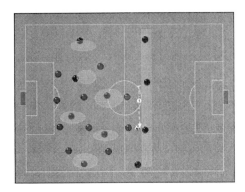

Exercise 5:

- Ball movement between the four defenders for ten seconds.
- The four midfielders and two strikers position themselves in the space provided by the opposing team at a distance of three to five metres from the nearest opponent.
- During these ten seconds, the players move depending on the position of the ball, keeping the distance between them and opposing defenders.
- Each movement of the defenders, in an attempt to reduce this distance, is followed by a corresponding movement to maintain the distance by repositioning. Stop. Each player stops in that position and re-evaluates the distance and movement during this period of time.
- Return to the starting positions, or continue from the current positions developed after ten seconds.

Exercise 6:

- Ball movement between the four defenders.
- At the signal, the ball comes into play, and the players keep possession of the ball using those four defenders as neutral players who cannot be dispossessed off the ball by the opposition.
- This exercise improves the players' positioning in the space provided at a distance of three to five metres from the nearest opponent, maintaining this distance for the duration of possession.

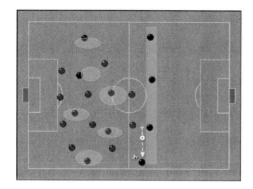

Exercise 7:

- Play an eleven versus eleven game.
- Start with a circulation of the ball between the four defenders, as a starting situation; then play normally on two goals. Return to starting position after a completed action, or if the game no longer falls under the proposed conditions.

C) When the Ball Is at the Midfield Line

How does the team play when the ball is at one of the players in the medial compartment? What are the defenders doing? What are the strikers, positioned in front of the ball, doing?

45

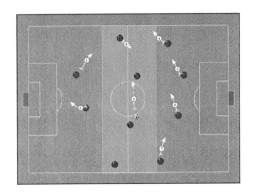

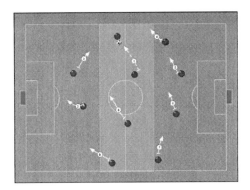

The team in possession of the ball develops a positional attack in the middle third of the field. The support compartments, both attackers and defenders, participate in horizontal shifting, offering the midfielders opportunities to link up and down.

Exercise 1:

- Isolated.
- Play with ten players. The team is positioned in the middle third of the field. The ball circulates between the players in the middle, who are organized in various types of 4-4-2.
- Each movement of the ball involves a corresponding movement of the players from the other lines. The forwards seek space and support possession. The defenders participate in maintaining possession, changing direction of play and when needed and receiving a pass back to release the pressure, which is usually created in the middle of the field.

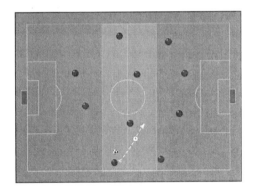

This exercise improves positional game for typical circulation patterns of the ball in the middle line. Positional play or play without the ball, depending on the position of the ball, is one of the greatest challenges of the zone play.

Exercise 2:

- Game conditions, phase of play.
- Play eleven versus eleven, one goal.
- The defending team is deployed in the middle third of the field.
- There is a neutral area for midfielders in possession of the ball, where the opponents can close down but cannot tackle.
- Attackers and defenders enter the horizontal shifting, offering solutions to keep possession. The game ends with a goal scored by the attacking team or when the ball is out of play. Repeat from the starting position (five actions).

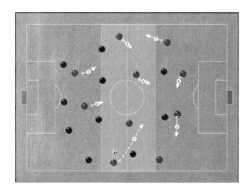

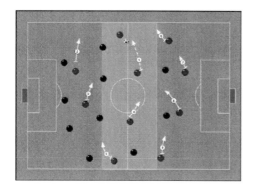

Placement and movement of the players are dependent on the movement of the ball, but also, on the position and movement of the opposing players. This continuous movement creates space needed to receive the ball and sustain possession, either through a pass back to the line of defenders or to the advanced line of attackers.

D) When the Ball Is at the Line of Attack

What do the players do behind the ball line? What are the midfielders and defenders doing if the attackers have to return the ball when they are up on the field in an advanced game situation?

49

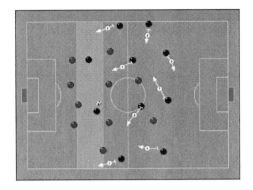

The situation is quite common, especially in positional attack when the team is deployed on the entire width of the pitch, in the opponent's half of the field. Midfielders and defenders, who are behind the ball, help to maintain possession through a horizontal motion depending on the ball position and space offered by the opposing team.

Training Methods

Exercise 1:

- Isolated game situation.
- Ball circulation in between the two strikers at thirty metres from the opposing goal. Each movement of the ball requires a shift of the players behind the ball in order to support ball possession.

Exercise 2:

- Game situation, ten versus ten. Positional play to a single goal.
- There is a neutral area for the attackers in possession.
- The team is initially positioned at thirty metres from the opposing goal. The strikers have their backs to the opposing goal and return the ball to players behind.
- Midfielders and defenders maintain possession through a horizontal shifting motion, depending on the position of the ball and playing spaces offered by the opposing team.
- The exercise ends with a goal scored, and then the players go back to the starting position (five actions).

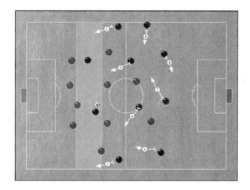

Attackers gain possession against opposing defensive line but lacking momentary solutions against a compact and well-placed defence, they are forced to return the ball to the midfield.

Keeping possession, supported by the midfielders and defenders, and then returning to attack in another area of the field seem to be a tactical solution for such a phase of play.

Vertical Shifting

Vertical shifting is that situation of the game when the ball is moving on the vertical axis of the field, leading to a corresponding vertical movement of the players and lines – and actually the whole team. There are two types of shifting.

- vertical shifting, which is done towards the opposing goal; in this book it is called positive shifting

- vertical shifting towards own goal, called negative shifting

Typical phases:
A) Moving ball on the right flank in depth forwards/backwards
B) Moving ball on the left flank in depth forwards/backwards
C) Moving ball in the central area in depth forwards/backwards
D) Moving ball diagonally forwards/backwards

There are two game situations.

1. The team is positioned behind the ball position.

There are situations of the game when the team is positioned in defence in the middle third, and one of the attackers manages an interception in the midfield area. The team is positioned currently behind the position where the ball was recovered by the attacker, and the team must quickly move vertically to support possession and occupy playing spaces offered by the opposing players.

2. The team is positioned in front of the ball position.

This tactical situation, when the team is positioned in front of the ball, is seen in every game. For instance, the team is positioned in defence and inside its own penalty box, and the goalkeeper holds the ball. At this time, the players move vertically towards that space that was previously occupied by the opponents and build their attack from the back.

Training Methods and Exercises for Vertical Shifting during Phase of Possession

a) Positive and negative vertical shifting of the defensive line

b) Positive and negative vertical shifting of the defensive and middle lines

c) Positive and negative vertical shifting of the defensive, middle, and attacking lines

From the methodological point of view, we divided the field into three areas of 35m to have a clearer analytical picture: 0–35m, defensive third; 35–70m, middle third; 70–105m, attacking third.

a) How does the team play when the ball moves vertically between 0–35m from its own goal?

This situation is common in different moments of the game, and it occurs both on the sides of the field and in the centre. First we train the vertical shifting of the defensive line, and then we add the midfield and the strikers' lines. There will be established a starting position and two points of reference, which are the typical cornerstones of developing the negative and positive vertical shifting of the players.

1) We train the defenders' line, who are positioned in relation to the initial position of the ball. The ball is passed to the advanced player, who is taken as a reference point. The three defenders find a new position according to the new position of the ball, ensuring that the possession is maintained and the attacking phase is being built up.

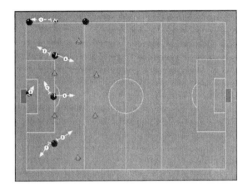

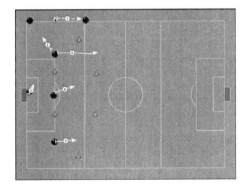

2) Once the line of defenders has learned the vertical shifting movement in the defensive third, then we can add

the midfield line. Use the same starting position and reference points as shown previously, in order to assemble these two lines for positive and negative vertical shifting. Repeat the response of the team.

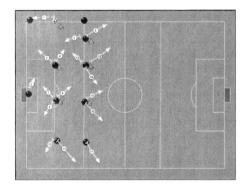

3) Finally, add the line of attack and repeat vertical shifting with the entire functional assembly of ten players.

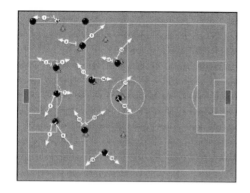

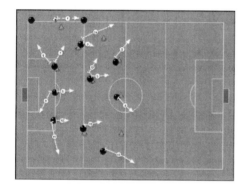

b) How does the team play when the ball moves vertically between 35–70m from its own goal?

We first train the vertical shifting of the defensive line, and then we add the line of midfielders and strikers. The coach sets the starting position and the two points of reference.

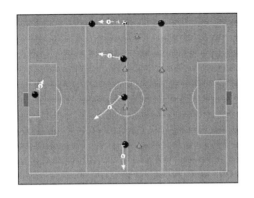

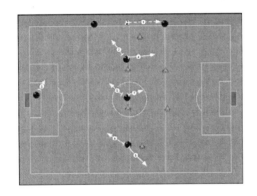

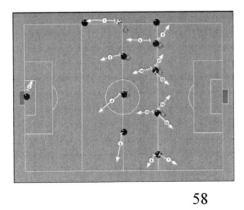

58

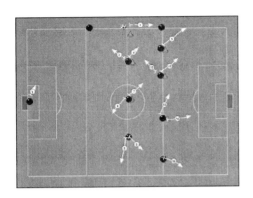

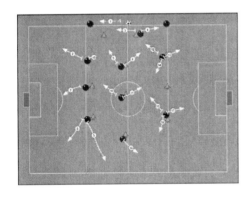

59

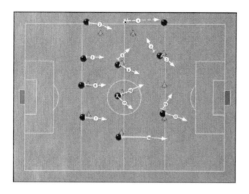

c) How does the team play when the ball moves vertically between 70–105m from its own goal?

We first train the vertical shifting of the defensive line, and then we add the line of midfielders and strikers. The coach sets the starting position and the two points of reference.

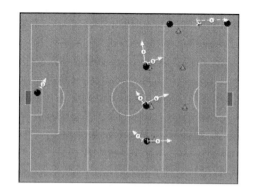

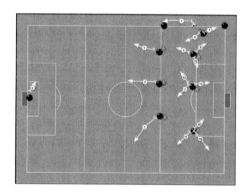

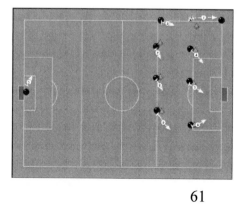

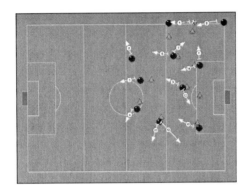

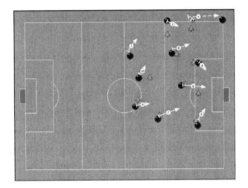

These two positions of the ball are points of reference for which we want to develop the players' tactical reaction during phase of possession. These positions of the ball are typical situations, and the possibility of being encountered in each game is relatively high. In this phase all the players participate actively, each player having more or less contribution depending on his position in relation to the ball.

Training Methods

Exercise 1:

- Small-sided games: five versus five with two neutral players on the right flank.
- Once one neutral player receives the ball, he plays a vertical pass to the other neutral player, who can cross or set in front of the goal to finish.

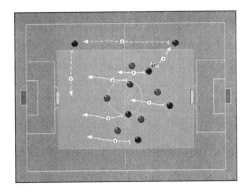

Exercise 2:

- Phase of play is eleven versus eleven, with two neutral players on one of the flanks.
- The role of the flank players is to facilitate the vertical movement of the ball.
- The team has to react accordingly in relation to this vertical movement of the ball.

63

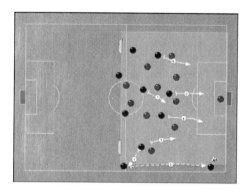

Phase of Non-possession (Defence)

Horizontal and Vertical Shifting during the Phase of Non-possession (Zone Defending)

In zone defending, the team is arranged in a compact, functional block and is required to keep the distance between lines, departments, and players depending on the path of the ball during opponents' attack. This compact arrangement of the entire functional unit is made through a shifting motion. A player's position in this type of organization remains the same, but he changes the area where he operates. For example, the right central defender will always be positioned between left central back and right back in a back four defence organization, but the area of the field where they activate may be different depending on the position of the ball.

Arrigo Sacchi said, "My zone was different. Marking was passed from player to player as the attacking player moved through different zones." Both defensive and attacking movement of the precision Milan achieved under Sacchi had never been seen before – those Rossoneri were tactical revolutionaries.

Horizontal Shifting

During horizontal shifting, the team moves as a compact block, keeping the distances between players and leaving the opposite side uncovered. By doing this sliding movement towards the position of the ball, the players will alternate their closing down, covering, marking, and double marking tasks. The player who is the closest to the ball has the responsibility to close down the opponent and stop the development of the game. The player from the immediate area has the responsibility to cover the player who comes out to close down, and possibly to mark any opponent who enters that respective zone. A detailed, analytical approach of the horizontal shifting during phase of non-possession allows all the players to learn what typical situations they will encounter in the game and their role play in these situations.

Methods of Training
1. Defensive line shifting
2. Defensive and middle lines shifting

3. Defensive, midfield, and attack assembly shifting

1) Defensive Line Shifting

- Isolated (no opposition).
- Variations of different defending organizations – four defenders, three defenders, five defenders – depending on the system of play.
- Defensive lines of one to four players; these are versions of zone defending that can be selected depending on the opponents or one's own players.
- Two to five points of reference of the ball position, creating typical game situations.

Exercise 1:

Use a displacement of four players to block a pass through the defending line towards the opposing player who stands behind the line. The player who is closest to the ball has the responsibility to close down, and the other three players are positioned on one or two defensive lines, taking on the duties of covering and marking. Maintaining a compact distance of ten to fifteen metres throughout the shift will result in releasing an area on the opposite side of the ball position. The farthest player from the ball has the task to cover this area in the event of a change of direction of play.

The other players will move horizontally, taking as a point of reference the new position of the ball, and they will readjust the distances and take over the tasks of covering and marking. In the progression, we can add two players in front of the defending line who play the role of the strikers.

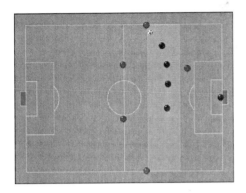

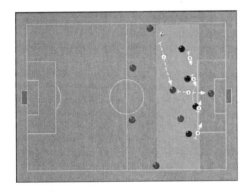

Exercise 2:

- Defensive line shifting, game situation, limited playing area.
- Four defenders, two strikers, four reference points of the ball, the goal defended by a goalie.

Defenders are shifting horizontally depending on ball position, and they change their roles such as closing down, covering, and marking in these four typical game situations created by the four reference points of the ball. Space limitation in this training situation means a possibility to train players on the horizontal shifting in a narrower area, thus focusing on alternative responsibilities caused by the movement of the ball and opposing players.

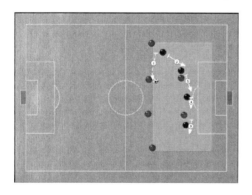

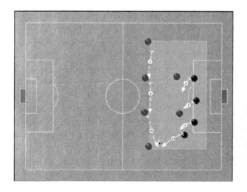

Exercise 3:

- Closing down, covering, and marking in zone play (without the ball).
- Four versus two in a designed area; the two strikers try to cross the defensive line of four defenders who are defending this limited space through specific movements such as closing down, covering, and marking.

The two strikers must try to go through and get an object that is placed behind the defensive line through motions of penetration, changes of direction, or individual tactical strategies – without coming in contact with opposing defenders. The tactical module, which consists of four defenders, will coordinate their movements so that the area is covered, without their movement paths being crossed.

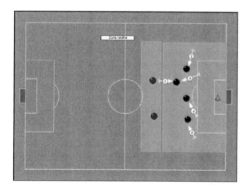

Strikers have a neutral zone in which they can withdraw, stepping away from the pressure of the defenders, and they will prepare a new attack on a new direction and in a different area. If the strikers are tagged by the defenders, they must return to the neutral zone, from where they can initiate a new attempt.

Horizontal Shifting of the Defensive Line and Middle

- Four defenders, two midfielders; four defenders and two wide midfielders; four defenders and four midfielders
- One to four defensive lines
- Two to five points of reference

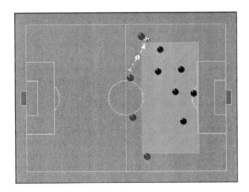

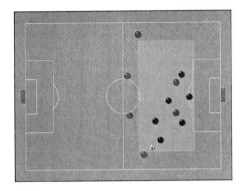

These points of reference will give the players the opportunity to respond, in terms of positional play, to a phase of play which they will encounter in the game. These positions of the ball create different typical game situations, at first on the left and then the right sides of the field. These positions of the ball are then established by analyzing previous matches when the team did not respond adequately. By limiting space, which minimizes the distances of shifting, the players will gain self-confidence and take on specific defending responsibilities with ease.

The two central midfield players alternatively take on tasks of closing down, covering, and marking in correlation with the defending line and the position of the ball.

Horizontal Shifting of the Defensive Line, Midfield, and Attack

- Four defenders, four midfielders, and two strikers
- One to four defensive lines

71

- Two to five points of reference

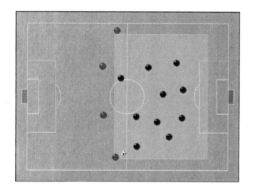

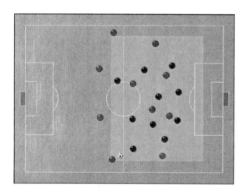

Positional response of the players will be trained with no opponents at first. Body position of the players, the distances between players, and the distances between lines are features that give the defence the final expected efficiency. Shifting horizontally and maintaining compact distances will result in uncovered spaces on the opposite side of the ball position; this task is taken by the player who is positioned farthest from the ball in case of a change of direction towards that previously inactive area.

Vertical Shifting

The ball position and its movement on the vertical axis of the field imply a vertical movement of the entire defensive block. From the direction of the movement point of view, there are two types of shifting: positive and negative.

- Positive – towards the opposition's goal in situations of advanced pressing in the opponent's half
- Negative – towards one's own goal in situations of deliberate or forced drop back

An effective vertical shifting means that each player knows his role and responsibilities very well and requires an analytical approach, section by section.

Training Methods

1. Vertical shifting of the defensive line

2. Vertical shifting of the defensive and middle lines

3. Vertical shifting of the defensive, middle, and attack lines

1. Vertical Shifting of the Defensive Line (Back Four)

a) Defensive Third, Four Defenders
- Two points of reference
- Passed ball, dribbled ball
- Without opposition
- Specific right-side movement, specific left-side movement

Ball Being Passed

From the starting position, the ball is moved vertically backwards. The defenders will change their positions and shift vertically in relation to this new position of the ball. Then they come back to the set starting position. The ball is moved forwards, and the defenders will shift vertically in relation to this position of the ball.

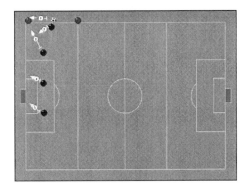

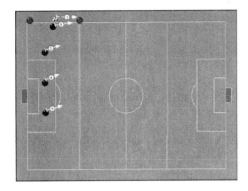

Dribbled Ball

The ball is driven towards the reference points. The defensive block will adopt a different organization compared to the previous situation, when the ball was being passed.

b) Middle Third, Four Defenders

- Starting position and two reference points
- Dribbled ball, passed ball

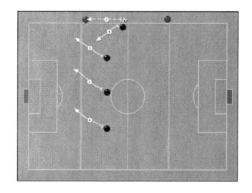

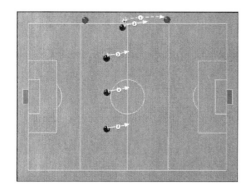

c) Attacking Third, Four Defenders

- Starting position and two reference points
- Passed ball
- Dribbled ball

76

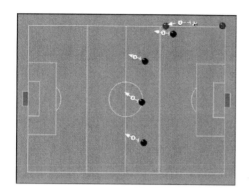

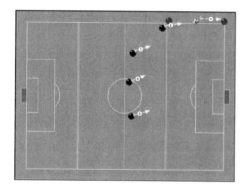

2. Vertical Shifting of the Defensive and Middle Lines

a) Defensive third, four defenders, four midfielders

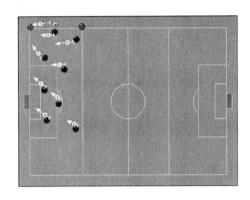

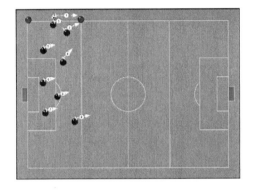

b) Middle third, four defenders, four midfielders

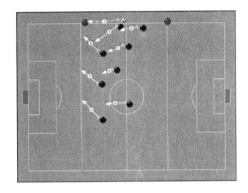

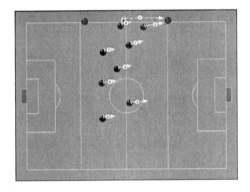

c) Attacking third, four defenders, four midfielders

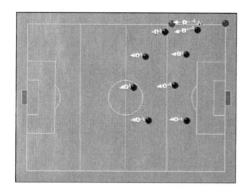

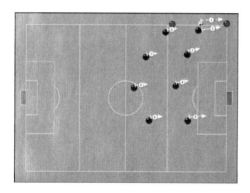

Vertical Shifting of the Defensive, Middle, and Attack Lines

a) Defensive third, four defenders, four midfielders, two attackers

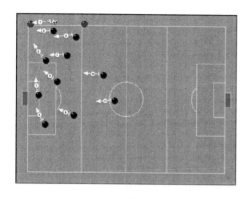

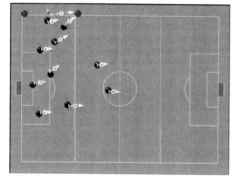

b) Middle third, four defenders, four midfielders, two attackers

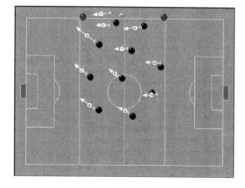

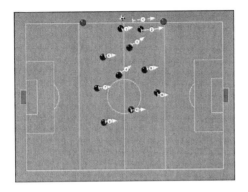

c) Attacking third, four defenders, four midfielders, two attackers

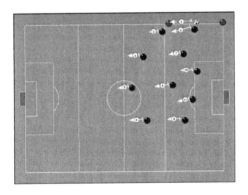

The Concept of Transition in the Game of Football

The transition is the temporal and spatial component of switching from one typical phase of the game to another. It could be a transition from attack to defence, from defence to attack, or within the same phase of play (switching from defence on the right to defence on the left side, or shifting from positional attack to finish in front of the goal from a cross, etc.).

"In preparation for the final match of the Champions League with AC Milan, Ajax training was based on improving rapid transition from defence to attack when they recover the ball in the midfield area" (Kormelink, Seveerens 1997, 90).

The game of football is analytically regarded as a succession of phases of the game. In football there are about 100–150 typical game phases. In the game, the typical phases follow each other in an order that can be somewhat anticipated. In between these typical situations, there will be encountered atypical phases when the players must react intuitively. Transition must be done quickly, accurately, and efficiently. As long as those two typical phases are executed separately and very well, the transition should not raise particular problems. Recognition of these phases in proper time is another requirement of effectiveness of the transition.

Examples of Transition:

a) attack-defence

b) defence-attack

c) attack-attack

d) defence-defence

Transition from Attack to Defence

The transition from attack to defence is a playing situation when possession of the ball is lost, and the team switches to the phase of recovery of the ball. Depending on where the ball is lost, the team reacts differently. Also, the development of the attack of a team is reflected on the transition to defence. For example, teams that prefer to play counterattack style will have a reduced transition because this type of team will drop back and stay compact.

If a team is carrying out a positional attack on the entire width of the field with players being positioned in all lines, the transition to defence will involve all players who took part in the attack.

Here is an analytical sequence of the transition moments.

1. Loss of possession

2. Attempt to recover the ball in six seconds by reducing the space towards the position of the ball

3. Organized zone defence

Transition from Defence to Attack

Transition from defence to the attack phase is a tactical game situation in which the ball is recovered in different areas of the field, and the team switches to a form of attack specific to that moment of the game. The reaction of the team to such a situation can be trained tactically, regarding the movement of the players and the time of transition from one phase to another.

Here is the analytical succession of the phases during transition from defence to attack.

1. Recover the ball.

2. Increase the distance between the player in possession and the other players.

3. Position players in the space provided by the opposing team.

Transition from Attack to Attack

This sequence is common during extended attacking phases of a team. The team switches from one attacking form to another depending on the development of the game. Lack of timing and coordination of all players involved in such a tactical situations requires a separate approach, and it needs to be trained in detail.

Examples

1) The transition from one form of attack to another:

- building from the back to fast attack
- fast attack to positional attack
- counterattack to positional attack
- unsuccessful finishing to rebuilding up from the back

2) Transition of attack from a certain area of the field to another area is determined by

- switching direction of play; and
- unsuccessful attack and resume play in a different area.

Transition from Defence to Defence

This transition is the switch from one form of defence to another or from one area of the field to another, respective to the game situation. There are many game situations that cause this type of transition.

- change of direction of attack
- recovery of the ball for a very short period of time, and the opposing team resumes the attack in another area
- clearing the attack for a short time and transition to defence in another area or another form

Quick succession of various attacking phases during the game will require the defending team to develop strategies to stop opponents to take initiative. Sometimes the defending team is forced to continuously do this transition for a longer period of time, depending on the duration of the attack.

Training Methods and Exercises for the Concept of Transition

Transition is the temporal and spatial dimension of switching from one typical phase to another. It may be switching from attack to defence or from defence to attack, or it can be within the same type of phase.

Transition from Attack to Defence

Methods and Exercises of Training:

These methods allow players to perceive the transition trigger (when), to minimize transition time (how long), and to clarify the movement of each player (where) in order to obtain a tactical advantage.

General Training Methods:

1. Outnumbered situations – with a starting position

2. Numerical superiority situations – with a starting position

3. Succession of sequences of two phases of the game (one sequence ends and another begins)

4. Second phase resulting from the second ball entered in the game by the coach

Method 1

An outnumbered situation that starts from a given starting position and uses a real game situation – namely, that the chances for the outnumbered team to lose possession of the ball are higher, which will trigger the transition in defence.

Exercise 1:

- One versus two, with goalkeeper and two small goals.
- The exercise begins with a pass to the player who is laterally on the goal line and initially plays the role as an attacker. He needs to score in one of two small goals.
- When he touches the ball, the other two players who are on the opposite side will begin to apply pressure, trying to recover the ball as quickly as possible.
- Once they have recovered the ball, both players switch to attack and can score in the big goal against the opposition of the other player, who becomes an active defender.
- The action ends when a goal has been scored or the ball is out of play.
- Resume from the starting position after a rotation of the players.

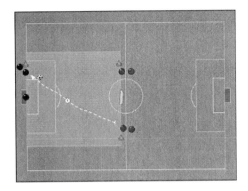

This exercise can be developed into an exercise of one on two, two on three, and three on four.

Method 2

Numerical superiority is a method in which the transition occurs due to the specific organization of the setup.

Exercise 1:

- Five on two, with a goalkeeper.

Four defenders and a defensive midfield player are positioned thirty metres away from their own goal, which is defended by the goalkeeper. Two opposing strikers are in line with the defenders. From this starting position the coach sends a pass back to the goalkeeper. At this point when the coach offers a pass back to the goalkeeper (which will happen in a real game situation), the four defenders and one midfielder, who were primarily positioned in defence, will aim at a fast transition from defence to a form of attack – in this case, building up from the back.

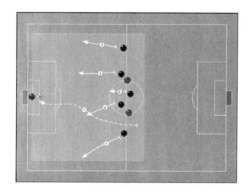

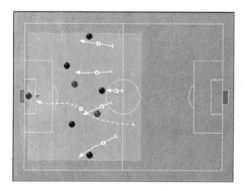

Territorial deployment of these five players plus one goalkeeper should initiate and facilitate possession and progressive advancement. It may be conditioned by introducing a number of passes the players need to make before scoring in a small goal or getting past the halfway line. The two strikers can win possession of the ball by pressing and then score in the big goal defended by the goalkeeper.

Here is another tactical transition moment of those five players, who must quickly switch from attack to defence.

Resume from the starting position when a goal has been scored or the ball is out of play. This exercise goes normally through two phases of the game, and you can continue to play for a certain period of time. Resume with the other two players in the middle. It can be developed in a six-on-three or seven-on-four drill. By adding a small goal for the team which has a numerical advantage, and by keeping the number of passes (ten), this exercise becomes a bilateral game in numerical superiority conditions, but with different goal sizes.

Through this method the players are trained to improve the ability to shift from one phase of play to another during situations of numerical superiority.

In this exercise, I am using a pass back and a starting position for two reasons: firstly, to encourage the strikers to apply pressure, and secondly, to create opportunities for progressive possession of the ball by playing from the goalkeeper.

By considering this idea of numerical superiority as a starting point, we can create different situations of transition similar to a realistic game situation, which can be improved in practice.

Method 3

Succession of sequences is a method that begins with a certain phase, and the end of this phase triggers the transition to another phase, which is actually the training objective. The coach must establish beforehand the tactical moment that will trigger the transition. These tactical moments are chosen from real game situations in order to promote understanding of the process of transition and its purpose. The second phase or action to which the transition is made is known by all the players in advance.

Exercise 1:

- One on one, two goals and a goalkeeper.

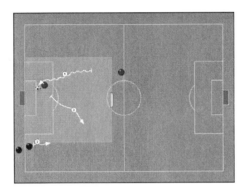

A player dribbles the ball and shoots on the goal. When this player shoots at the goal, a second player starts dribbling the ball to the opposing goal from a predetermined position, to score. Switching from attack to defence must be fast, allowing the first player to recover the second ball in play and finish a second action with the opposition of the second player, who will switch to defence. The action will end when one or two goals have been scored or the ball goes out.

Exercise 2:

- Eleven versus eleven.

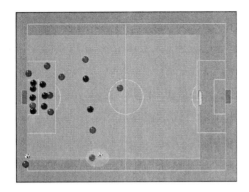

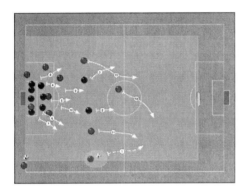

- Sequence 1: the team is organized in attack for a corner kick.
- Sequence 2: counterattack by the defending team through player B1, who is positioned at twenty metres from his own goal near the sideline.
- Transition trigger moments to sequence 2: a goal has been scored, the ball goes out of play, or the defending team clears away a corner kick ball.

Red team is switching from attack to defence, trying to recover the ball as quickly as possible (six seconds), and closer to the opposing goal. The action ends with a goal or when the ball is out of play. This exercise can be repeated starting from the initial position. The teams switch roles after five or six turns.

Method 4

A second phase is introduced by the second ball.

Exercise 1:

- Eleven versus eleven; bilateral game.

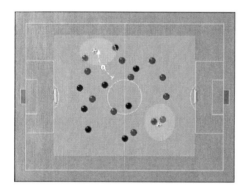

Blue team is training on shifting rapidly from one phase to another (attack to defence). The transition is triggered by the introduction of the second ball by the coach in certain situations of the game. The team has to switch from the development of the previous action to the second phase introduced by the new ball. The objectives of such a tactical exercise are to train the availability of the players who switch quickly from one situation to the next one, to develop the ability to read the new situation, and to solve a new tactical task in limited time.

Transition from Defence to Attack

The team can be trained regarding the movement of the players and the time of transition from one phase to another.

General training methods:

1. Outnumbered situations
2. Numerical superiority situations
3. Succession of sequences
4. Second phase introduced by a second ball

These training methods of transition, mentioned previously in the transition from attack to defence, can be applied to the transition from defence to attack as well, but the focus is on the player or group from team B. The transition drills provide a simultaneous, two-phase approach (attack-defence, defence-attack), and these sequences can only be separated from the teaching point of view.

Transition from Attack to Attack

This succession of two attacking sequences is common during an extended possession phase of a team. The players switch from one attacking situation to another depending on the development of the game.

Examples:

- Building up, to attack in front of the goal

- Fast attack, to attack position
- Counterattack, to attack position
- Attack in front of the goal, to building up from the goalkeeper

Example 1:

- Transition from the building-up phase to a rapid attack on the opposite side.

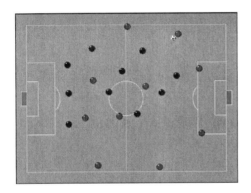

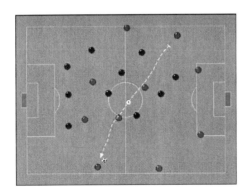

98

This is a typical tactical situation encountered by the teams in the building-up phase of the game, which starts in their own defensive third of the field. These are two different types of attack that can be connected through a rapid transition to create an advantage in that area.

Example 2:

- Transition from positional attack to building up, with the goalkeeper having the ball for the second sequence.

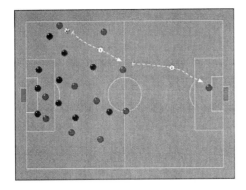

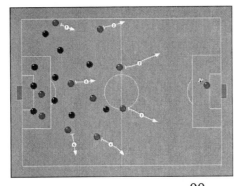

A rejected positional attack can lead the attacking team to a position from where the players have to resume the phase of attack even if the ball goes back to their own goalkeeper.

This type of transition between two forms of attack can be anticipated in practice, both in terms of players' movements and the effective time they need to perform.

Example 3:

- Transition from counterattack to positional attack.

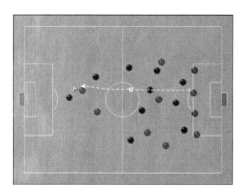

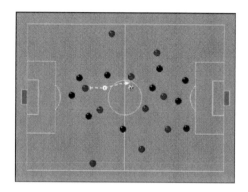

A logical, progressive succession of two sequences in the normal attacking development of the game should not raise problems in practice and game. These tactical sequences are succeeding in the opposite direction of a normal progression of the game; for example, a counterattack blocked by the opposing team, which will be shifted to a positional attack, requires a separate analysis and approach in training.

Training Methods

Method 1: Succession of Sequences

Exercise 1:

- One on one, a single goal.
- Player A has the ball and tries to score in the duel.

If he scores, the ball goes out of bounds, or he loses possession of the ball, the coach will give a second ball to the attacking player for a second attack from a different angle. The attacking player shifts from one sequence, which in this case is the first attack, to a second sequence, the second attack, which will be initiated from a different area. This type of drill can be developed for two on two, three on three, and small-sided games.

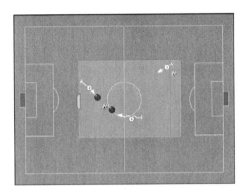

Exercise 2:

- Eleven versus eleven, one goal.

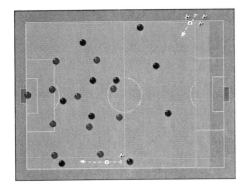

- Sequence 1: positional attack.
- Sequence 2: building up begins from the right side.
- Moments of transition: loss of possession, goal scored, ball out.

The attacking team's players change the positions that they had for the first attack and begin the second attack, taking as a point of reference the new position of the ball, which is determined beforehand. This exercise is realistic if it is based on an analysis of game situations encountered during previous matches. The final moment of an attacking action is determined and made known to all the players, and then it is connected to the second action, which is different from the first one.

Method 2: The Second Ball Introduced by the Coach for the Second Phase

Exercise 1:

103

In a bilateral game, various forms of attack will succeed because of the natural flow of the game. When the coach stops an ongoing phase by introducing a second ball into play, he actually directs the game into a new tactical situation and decides the number of repetitions and the pace of training.

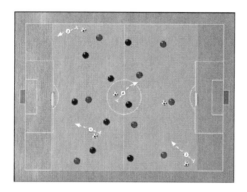

This type of transition from attack in a certain area of the field to attack in another area refers to the same type of attack, but it takes place successively in two to three areas of the field. It is determined by

- switching the play;
- resuming a rejected attack in a different area; and
- losing possession for a short period of time and resuming the attack in another area.

Diverse forms and directions of attack will make the opponents lose their organization and finally give space to the opposing players.

Training Methods

Method 1: Succession of Sequences

Exercise 1:

- Five versus five, one goal, opponent's half.
- Sequence 1: attacking team has possession of the ball.
- Sequence 2: attacking team resumes a second attack in a different area of the field, which was previously established.
- Transition trigger: loss of possession, goal scored. or ball goes out.

There's a limited time for transition (four seconds). Red team has five to six successive attacking actions, which are initiated from different areas, and the players are seeking for solutions to finish.

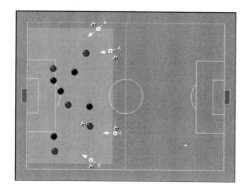

Exercise 2:

- Eleven versus eleven, using two-thirds of the field.
- Starting position: right back plays on from a wide pre-established position; red team is arranged defensively in the middle third so as to win the ball back as soon as possible.
- Sequence 1: blue team is playing to score from a ball initiated by the right back.
- Sequence 2: blue team is playing to score from a ball initiated from the left side.
- Transition trigger: loss of possession, goal scored, or ball goes out.

Changing direction of play requires refocusing the attack on the opposite side in an area of the field that was relatively inactive. This new position of the player who has possession of the ball requires support from teammates who were first positioned to support the first attack. Quick transition to this new situation and participation of all the players to support this new area of attack will create a territorial and numerical advantage, which is the tactical purpose of the zone play.

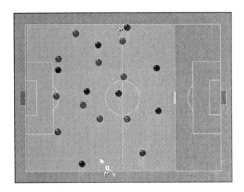

Method 2: A Second Ball Introduced by the Coach for the Second Phase

This training method will give the coach the freedom to choose the right time and right area in which to introduce the second ball. Thus, the coach deliberately creates certain attacking situations in certain areas – situations that must first be recognized by the players and then done according to the team's predetermined, tactical plan. A team that proves tactical flexibility, especially in such situations of transition in various areas, will create a numerical and territorial advantage that will unbalance the opponent's defence.

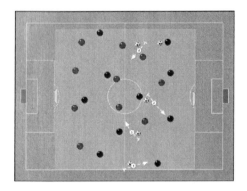

Transition from Defence to Defence

This transition is a game situation specifically used during prolonged attacks by the opposing team. The team in defence has to respond continuously and appropriately by displaying different forms of defence, and most of the time in different areas.

1) Transition from Defence in One Area of the Field to Another

Example:

Changing the direction of play by the opposing team to the opposite side of the field will require a transition in time and space of the entire defending block to the other side, as well as reorganization of the defence for the new situation.

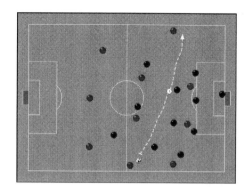

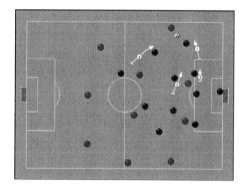

2) Transition between Two Different Forms of Organization of Defence

Example:

A team organized man to man defensively at a corner kick on the left rejects the attack at first, but the ball gets to the right side to the opposing team players, who will initiate another attack from that side. The defending team has to switch quickly from one form of organization (man to man) to another (zone-mixed), corresponding to the newly developed situation.

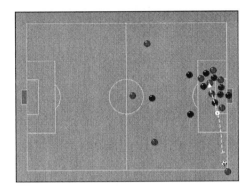

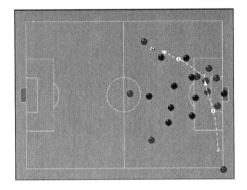

Recognizing these two different tactical situations and rapidly transitioning, in time and space, the whole defending ensemble to a new organizational form (sometimes completely different from the previous one) is the content of a training transition drill.

Method 1: Succession of Sequences

Exercise 1:

- Five versus five, one goal.
- Sequence 1: zone defending on the left side.
- Sequence 2: defending in front of the goal against a cross from the right side.
- Transition trigger: the ball is intercepted by the defending team.

A player from the opposing team is placed beforehand on the other side, ready to cross the ball. These five players, the back four and a defending midfielder, must change their initial defensive positions and reposition themselves in the shortest time possible, so as to stop the attacking action from the opposite side.

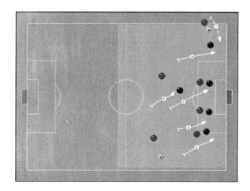

Exercise 2:

- Eleven versus eleven, half of the field
- Sequence 1: zone defence in the middle third of the field organized in the central area.
- Sequence 2: defending against an attack initiated through a long diagonal ball from the right or left side.
- Transition trigger: the defending team intercepts ball centrally in the first phase.

Changing the direction of play can create problems when the defending team is surprised by such executions.

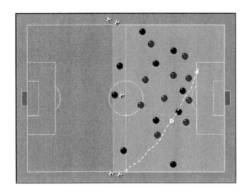

Method 2: Second Ball Introduced by the Coach

Exercise 1:

A second ball is put into play in different areas at the right moment, chosen by the coach. The team's flexibility is evident in such situations when players on defence must shift easily from one phase to another by changing the type of defensive organization.

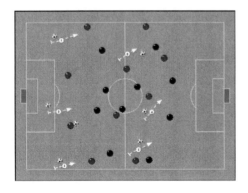

The football game can be seen as a succession of sequences of play, both in defence and in attack. These moments of transition from one phase to another are often regarded as the critical tactical situations during which breakdowns occur in system organization.

Conclusions

Let's return to the original question, which was the starting point and motivation for this book: Are the players' technical and tactical knowledge and skills influenced by the requirements of the zone play? Any modification of the game – meaning tactical progress, which automatically requires changes at the technical level – should have consequences on the technical and tactical early training period of the players. Ninety percent of teams that play top-level football have a playing philosophy based on zone play or variants of it. FC Barcelona is the ideal model of organization based on zone play.

In terms of zone play's concepts and their applicability in children and juniors' training I have drawn the following conclusions:

The concept of transition has a very motivating response from the children, even from the ages of nine and ten years.
The space is perceived with reticence at first, but then the perception of the distance from player to the ball and from player to player gradually improves. The first sign of understanding of the concept of space is when not all the players are placed around the ball.

Time is not perceived with ease at young ages, but the training is making remarkable progress.
Shifting in all its forms is introduced in the possession and positional play drills. Because the children's attention is still largely kept on the ball, the development of field orientation in relation to other landmarks – teammates, opponents, opposing goal – is not an easy task.

116

The zone play concepts can be introduced in the juniors' training sessions from the ages of nine and ten, and then perfected until the age of eighteen, when they are promoted to the senior team.

The following is an example of a weekly training program including all four zone play concepts.

Monday	Tuesday	Wednesday	Thursday	Friday	Saturday	Sunday
Space	Time	Transition	Shifting	Time	Shifting	
Time	Space	Shifting	Transition	Space	Transition	
		Space			Time	Match

Match Analysis

Real Madrid vs. Borussia Dortmund – Champions' League group games (6.11.2012)

Real Madrid's way of playing was analyzed from the four zone play concepts point of view: space, time, shifting, and transition.

Space

Space in Phase of Possession:

The Distance between the Players Who Receive the Ball and Their Nearest Opponents

First Half

Player	0-1m	1-2m	2-3m	3-4m	4-5m	5m+	Total
Albeloa	1	1	3			22	27
Varane				1		23	24
Pepe			2			18	20
Ramos		3	3	1	1	29	37
Alonso	1	4	10	2	2	7	26
Modrici	1	7	9	4	2	15	38
Ronaldo	9	4	9	5	3	4	34
Di Maria	5	1	9	2	1	7	25
Higuain	1	2	1	1			5
Ozil	1	6	5	3	1		16
Total	19	28	51	19	10	125	252

Notes:

- The most number of balls received: Ramos (37), Modrici (38), and Ronaldo (34).
- The least number of balls received: Higuain (5).
- There were players who received the ball at a distance greater than 5 metres (125) from the nearest defender; Albeloa, Pepe, Varane, and Ramos who did that 96 times.
- Positional play shows that the players received the ball at a distance of 0–1 metres from the nearest defender just 19 times, and Ronaldo accounted for 9 of them.

Questions:

- Why did Ramos receive the ball 29 times in a free space (+5 metres) without pressure?
- Why did Higuain receive the ball only 5 times?
- Why did Ronaldo receive the ball 9 times in tight situations (0–1 metres)?

Second Half

Notes:

- The most number of balls received: Ramos (35), Alonso(34), and Essien (37).
- The least number of balls received: Ronaldo (27) and Callejon (25).
- The number of balls received at a distance of +5 metres from the nearest defender: 74 (52 of them by the defenders).
- The tightest situations belong to Ronaldo, with 9 times in less than 1 metre of space.
- Other players received the ball in a 1–2 metre space: Di Maria (14), Callejon (11), Ozil (10).

Questions:

- What could the players do to find more space?

- Is there any way the players could avoid these tight situations?

Player	0-1m	1-2m	2-3m	3-4m	4-5m	5m+	Total
Albeloa	1	3	5	1		10	20
Varane		1	1			15	17
Pepe	2	3	5	2	2	15	29
Ramos		1	9	5	8	12	35
Alonso	7	10	5	3	5	4	34
Essien	4	9	3	9	5	7	37
Ronaldo	9	1	11	4	1	1	27
Di Maria	5	14	7	1	2	2	31
Callejon	2	11	5	4	1	2	25
Ozil	3	10	8	3	4	1	29
Kaka	3	4					7
Total	36	67	59	32	28	74	296

Space in Phase of Non-possession

The Distance between Opposition Players Who Receive the Ball and Real's Nearest Defender

First Half

Zone	Time	0-1m	1-2m	2-3m	3-4m	4-5m	5m+	Total
1/3D	0-15'	3	4	4	2	1	3	17
	15-30'			1 (goal)				1
	30-45'	6	4	3 (goal)		1		13
1/3 M	0-15'	10	8	7	6	2	12	45
	15-30'	10	10	7	5	4	15	51
	30-45'	6	9	6	3	2	2	29
1/3 A	0-15'		5	1	2		6	14
	15-30'	4	3	5	2	3	3	21
	30-45'	1		1	1		4	7
Total		40	43	35	21	13	45	197

Notes:

- The opponents received the ball 197 times.
- The most number of balls received (45) were at a distance of +5 metres.

- There were 40 situations when the ball was received in tight areas (0–1 metres).
- In Real's defensive third, the opponent received the ball 31 times.
- The space needed in Real's defensive third by the opponents to score both goals was less than 2–3 metres.
- It was a tight game in the middle third, with 125 balls received by the opponents, and 53 situations in a space less than 2 metres.

Zone	Time	0-1m	1-2m	2-3m	3-4m	4-5m	5m+	Total
1/3D	0-15	3		2			1	6
	15-30	3	2	1	2		5	13
	30-45	6	2	3		1	4	16
1/3 M	0-15	12	13	8	4	1	14	52
	15-30	16	4	10	3	3	5	41
	30-45	8	4	5	3	1	2	23
1/3 A	0-15	2	4	3	2		2	13
	15-30		3	1	2		1	7
	30-45	1	4	2	2		2	11
Total		50	36	35	18	6	36	181

Second Half

Notes:

- The opponents received the ball 181 times.
- The most number of balls received (50) was in a space less than 1 metres.
- There were 10 situations when the opposition received the ball in a +5 metre space in the defensive third.
- There was no advanced pressure in the attacking third, because the opposition had the ball for 31 times with 11 situations when they had 3–5 metres space to play.

- There were 106 balls received by the opposition in the middle third, with 26 situations when they had a space of 4–5 metres.

Time

Time in the Phase of Possession

Notes:

- The number of passes backwards in a game shows that the team in possession had to delay the attacking action and give more time to the players who are in front of the ball to find their receiving position; any pass back means more time given to the other players.
- There were 296 passes during the first half.
- 114 passes were backwards (47 percent).

Real Madrid-Borrussia Dormunth	Total number of passes	Passes forward	Passes backward	Conclusions
45min (first half)	296	159	114	47% backward passes

Shifting

Shifting in the Phase of Possession
Horizontal Shifting
First Half

Time 1	Who is passing	Back four action	Middle players action	Attackers action	Outcome
0.13	Modrici -Alonso	V		V	-keeping possession
0.28	Varane_Pepe		V	V	-Possession
0.52	Alonso-Albeloa		V	V	-Switching play-repositioning
5.18	Modrici -Ramos		V	V	-occupying space
5.23	Modrici -Alonso	V		V	-possession, adjusting positions
5.39	Varane-Pepe		V	V	-repositioning
8.04	Ramos-Modrici			V	-occupying space
8.17	Varane-Albeloa		V	V	-Switching play, possession
8.28	Pepe-Varane		V	V	-repositioning
11.51	Ramos-Varane-Albeloa		V	V	-Possession
12.11	Ramos-Modrici		V	V	-repositioning, Quick attack
14.55	Modrici-Albeloa		V	V	-repositioning
16.21	Modrici-Ramos		V	V	-repositioning
17.46	Albeloa-Varane-Ramos		V	V	-Occupying space,possession
18.01	Pepe-Modrici		V	V	-Finding space, possession
18.10	Ramos-Albeloa			V	-Dropping back to receive

130

Time 1	Who is passing	Back four action	Middle players action	Attackers action	Outcome
20.15	Ramos-Pepe		V	V	-repositioning, possession
20.29	Pepe -Ramos		V	V	-Space, possession
21.00	Varane-Pepe		V	V	-building up
22.06	Modrici-Ramos		V	V	-repositioning, possession
24.43	Ramos-Pepe-Modrici-Ramos	V	V	V	-repositioning, possession
28.10	Maria-Alonso-Modrici-Ramos	V	V	V	-occupying space, possession
28.45	Modrici-Ramos	V		V	-repositioning, possession
29.07	Pepe-Varane-Ramos		V	V	-Finding space, dropping back
29.22	Varane-Pepe-Varane		V	V	-building up
30.10	Modrici-Varane-Ramos		V	V	-Space-possession
31.12	Alonso-Ramos –Maria-Ramos-Pepe		V	V	-keeping possession
32.21	Albeloa-Ramos	V	V	V	-possession
36.15	Pepe-Varane		V	V	-posinioning
36.35	Pepe- Varane		V	V	-doping back to receive
36.51	Modrici-Albeloa		V	V	-possession
39.32	Modrici-Pepe-Varane-Ramos	V	V	V	-building up
41.15	Modrici-Varane-Ramos		V	V	-repositioning, possession
41.34	GK has the ball	V	V	V	-building up

Notes:

- There were 34 situations in the first half when the team was shifting horizontally in the phase of possession.
- The shift was a result of the horizontal movement of the ball and involved the lines in front of the ball.
- The purpose of this horizontal shifting was keeping possession and occupying a more advantageous space in the opponents' defensive lines.

Vertical Shifting (Positive, Negative; First Half) in the Phase of Possession

Time 1	Zone 1	Zone 2	Who is passing	Back four action	Middle players action	Attackers action	Outcome
00.43	1/3 M	1/3 A	Varane-Ronaldo	-push up	5m vertical repositioning	repositioning	quick prog
2.49	1/3 M	1/3 D	Ramos-Pepe	-repositioning	Negative shifting	Negative shifting	possession
15.12	1/3 M	1/3 A	Modrici -Ozil	-repositioning	Ronaldo's movement	repositioning	-getting bel 4
18.25	1/3 M	1/3 A	Alonso-Maria	repositioning	repositioning		-Possession -Scoring op
21.00	1/3M	1/3A	Ramos-Higuain		Ronaldo's movement in front of the goal		-scoring op
22.37	1/3 D	1/3 A	Ozil --Ronaldo's dribble		Maria's vertical mov	Higuain's vertical mov.	-scoring op
23.52	1/3 M	1/3 A	Alonso-Ozil		Maria, Ronaldo vertical shift	Higuain's vertical movement	-scoring op
25.43	1/3 D	1/3 A	Maria-Ronaldo	repositioning	Modrici, Ozil vertical movement	Higuain's vertical movement	Scoring op
31.05	1/3 M	1/3 A	Ramos-Ronaldo	Push up	Maria Ozil vertical shifting		Push up , p
32.31	1/3 M	1/3 A	Ramos-Ronaldo (diagonal pass)	Repositioning			-Possession
36.36	1/3M	1/3 D	Alonso-Pepe	Negative shifting			maintaining possession
39.50	1/3 M	1/3 A	Modrici-Maria	Repositioning			-scoring op
40.47	1/3 M	1/3 A	Ronaldo's Dribbling	Pushing up	repositioning		Progression opposition
43.25	1/3 D	1/3M	GK-Ramos	Pushing up and wide	Repositioning		Building up possession
43.32	1/3 M	1/3 A	Modrici-Ronaldo			Higuain's vertical move	Scoring op

Notes:

- There were 15 phases of play when the team was involved in a vertical shifting action.
- There were 2 negative vertical shifting actions that had an outcome of maintaining possession of the ball.

- Most of the time the receiver of the ball in the advanced lines was Ronaldo.
- There were 7 vertical shifting situations that led to scoring opportunities.

Shifting in the Phase of Non-possession
Horizontal Shifting (First Half)

Time 1	Ball zone	Back four action	Middle players action	Attackers action	Outcome
1.07	1/3M	v			Winning the ball back
6.03	1/3M	v	v		Winning the ball back
9.05	1/3 M	v	v		
9.10	1/3A	v	v	v	Defensive organization
19.31	1/3 M	v	v		
19.50	1/3 M	v	v		
20.01	1/3 D	v	v		
22.11	1/3 A	v	v		Winning the ball in 1/3 M
22.32	1/3 D	v	v		
25.35	1/3 D	v	v		Winning the ball, counterattack
26.21	1/3 M	v	v		
26.26	1/3 D	v	v		
30.27	1/3 A	v	v		
39.14	1/3 D	v			Winning the ball back by GK
44.14	1/3 A	v	v	v	Conceding goal

Notes:

- There were 15 game situations when the team had to shift horizontally in relation to the ball's horizontal movement.
- Most of the time the defensive back four and the middle players were involved in the shift.
- The distance between the players was 10–15 metres, maintaining tight lines and being aggressive.
- There were 13 game situations when the middle players were positioned behind the ball and got involved in the horizontal shifting.

Vertical Shifting (First Half)

Time 1	Area	Flank/Central	Pass/Driven	Back four action	Middle players action	Attackers action	Outcome
14.17	M 1/3	Central	Pass	V	V	V	Positive shifting Pushing up to occupy space
16.08	M 1/3	Central	pass	V	V		Dropping back for a deep pass
16.37	M 1/3	Right flank	pass	V	V		Long pass adjustment Won possession
17.40	D 1/3	Central – Free Kick	pass	V	V	V	Free kick long ball Adjusting distances
19.55	M 1/3	Central	driven	V	V	V	-Player penetration -8v5
27.06	M 1/3-D 1/3	Left flank	pass	V	V late		-long pass over the middle, deflection beh back 4 for a mid coming from a second lir 3v3 (goal)
29.39	M 1/3-D 1/3	Right flank	driven	V	V		-5v3
30.32	M 1/3	Right flank	driven	V	V		Flank penetration 6v5
35.18	D 1/3	Central free kick	pass	V	V		Long ball free kick clearance
35.22	M 1/3	Central	pass	V	V	V	Pass back-push up Positive shifting
37.29	M 1/3	central	pass	V	V		Pass through middle Narrowing space
39.09	M 1/3	central	pass	V	V		Long pass from the GK Dropping to deny space
42.35	M 1/3- D 1/3	Central	driven	V	V		Penetration through lines 6v3 Deny space wan ball back
42.58	A 1/3-M 1/3 –D 1/3	Left flank	Driven ,pass	V	V	V	Penetration left flank 6v4 getting in line with the ball
44.15	A 1/3	central	pass		V	V	Pass back-push up Positive shifting
44.17	A 1/3-D 1/3	central	pass	V	V		Long pass from the GK Late shifting, 6v3, (goal)

Notes:

- There were 31 vertical shifting situations in the phase of non-possession during the first half.
- There were 5 out of 31 situations of positive shifting.

- The majority of the actions took place or started in the middle third.
- The back 4 and middle 2 most often shifted negatively, towards their own goal.
- The trigger of the shifting movements were long passes and individual vertical runs on the flanks.

Transition

Attack-Defence

Notes:

There were 37 transition phases from attack to defence during the first half.

Defence-Attack (Second Half)

Notes:

There were 36 transitional phases from defence to attack during the second half.

Attack-Attack (Second Half)

Zone 1	Zone 2	Form of attack1	What trigger	Form of attack 2	Players action	Outcome
1/3 A-Corner	1/3 M	Corner Kick	Clearance	Positional attack	Repositioning dropping back	Keeping possession
1/3 A	1/3 M	Attacking in front of the goal	Clearance	2nd Attack	repositioning	Keeping possession
1/3 A	1/3 M	Attack inside the box	Back pass	Positional attack	repositioning	Keeping possession
1/3 M	1/3 M	Positional attack-right	Diagonal pass	Positional attack-left	repositioning	Keeping possession
1/3 M	1/3 M	Positional attack Left	Switching play	Positional attack -right	Repositioning	Possession-scoring opportunity
1/3 A	1/3 D	Attack in front of the box	Temporary loss of possession	Building up from the GK	repositioning	Possession Scoring opportunity
1/3 M	1/3 A	Positional attack-left	Switching play	Positional attack-right	repositioning	possession
1/3 A	1/3 M	Attack in front of the goal	Clearance	2nd attack from the right back	Repositioning Dropping back	Possession Scoring opportunity
1/3 A corner	1/3 M	Corner in attack	Clearance	2nd attack from the CB	repositioning	possession
1/3 A	1/3 M	Attack in front of the box	clearance	2nd attack from the left back	repositioning	Possession Goal opportunity
1/3 A	1/3 M	Attack in the box	Clearance	2nd attack from the CB	repositioning	Possession Free kick
1/3 A	1/3 M	Free Kick	Clearance	2nd attack from the CB	repositioning	Possession Goal opportunity
1/3 A	1/3 D	Attack in front of the box	clearance	Building up from the GK	repositioning	possession

Notes:

- The team was exposed to 13 game situations during the second half when the organization of the team had to switch from one form of attack to another.
- The transition was triggered by diverse tactical moments such as temporary clearance of the ball, switching play, or pass back.

139

- Most of the actions had an outcome of keeping possession and creating scoring opportunities.
- The team had a good sense of a second attack, with all the players reacting positively by repositioning themselves and keeping the energy of the attacking phase.
- Some of the second attacking phases had to restart from the goalkeeper or central defenders, which implied a whole team repositioning by dropping back from the advanced spaces gained in the previous attack.

Defence-Defence

1	Zone 1	Zone 2	Form of defence 1	What trigger	Form of defence 2	Players action	Outcome/pictures
	1/3 M	1/3 D	5v3 middle	Pass through	5v3 defence	Shifting vertically	
	1/3 M right side	1/3 D left side	10v10	Switching play	4v1 left side	Shifting horizontally	
	1/3 A	1/3 D	Advanced pressure in 1/3 A	counterattack	8v4 defence in front of the goal	8 players Shifting vertically	
	1/3 M left	1/3 M right	8v4 left side	Switching play	8v6 right side	Shifting horizontally	Winning the ball back
	1/3 M right	1/3 D left	9v9	Switching play	4v3 in the box	Shifting horizontally	Goal by opposing team
	1/3 M left	1/3 M central	Def free kick- left	clearance	Organized defence in 1/3 M	repositioning	Regain ball possession
	1/3 A left	1/3 D	Defending at a throw in	Miss pressing Quick attack	Defending in front of the goal	Shifting vertically	
	1/3 A	1/3 D	Defending 10v10 Gk has the ball	Long ball by the GK	Defending 4v3 in front of the goal	Back 4 wrong decision	Goal by the opposing team

Notes:

- There were 8 situations during the first half when the team had to make a transition from one form of defence to another.
- The transition was triggered by different game situations such as switching play, clearance, or misjudged pressure upfront.

141

- The goals were scored during this transition time from one form of defence to another.
  - At minute 27 the team was first in a 9 vs. 9 defensive situation with the ball on the right side, and it had to switch to different forms of defensive organization due to an extended ball possession by the opposing team. The final situation was a 4 vs. 3 in front of the box, with a player breaking through from the second line after a deflected ball by one of the strikers.
  - At minute 44 the team was first organized in a 10 vs. 10 situation, well positioned with the ball at the opposing goalkeeper. After a long ball made by the goalkeeper, the team had to switch to a 4 vs. 3 situation in front of the box. This was a similar action with an opposing player penetrating from the second line after a deflected ball by one of the strikers.

Bibliography

Kormelink, H., and T. Seeverens. 1997. *The Coaching Philosophies of Louis van Gaal and the Ajax Coaches.* Leeuwaarden, the Netherlands: Editura De Voetbal Trainer.

Kormelink, H., and T. Seeverens. 1997. *Team Building.* Leeuwaarden, the Netherlands: Editura De Voetbal Trainer.

Lucchesi, M. 2003. *Pressing.* Michigan: Editura Reedswain Publishing.

Marziali, F., and Vincenzo Mora. 2003. *The Zone: Advantages, Disadvantages, Countermeasures.* Michigan: Editura Reedswain Publishing.

Michels, R. 2001. *Team Building: The Road to Success.* Michigan: Editura Reedswain Publishing.

Railo, W., and H. Matson. 2001. *Sven Goran Eriksson on Soccer.* Michigan: Editura Reedswain Publishing.

Smink, J. 2004. *Ajax Training Sessions.* Michigan: Editura Reedswain Publishing.

Trapattoni, G. 1999. *Coaching High Performance Soccer.* Michigan: Editura Reedswain Publishing.

Vermeulen, H. 2003. *Zone Soccer: A Game of Time and Space.* Michigan: Editura Reedswain Publishing.